MIGHTY MACHINES

Trucks

by Mary Lindeen

BELLWETHER MEDIA · MINNEAPOLIS, MN

Note to Librarians, Teachers, and Parents:

Blastoff! Readers are carefully developed by literacy experts and combine standards-based content with developmentally appropriate text.

Level 1 provides the most support through repetition of high-frequency words, light text, predictable sentence patterns, and strong visual support.

Level 2 offers early readers a bit more challenge through varied simple sentences, increased text load, and less repetition of high-frequency words.

Level 3 advances early-fluent readers toward fluency through increased text and concept load, less reliance on visuals, longer sentences, and more literary language.

Whichever book is right for your reader, Blastoff! Readers are the perfect books to build confidence and encourage a love of reading that will last a lifetime!

This edition first published in 2007 by Bellwether Media.

No part of this publication may be reproduced in whole or in part without written permission of the publisher. For information regarding permission, write to Bellwether Media Inc., Attention: Permissions Department, Post Office Box 1C, Minnetonka, MN 55345-9998.

Library of Congress Cataloging-in-Publication Data
Lindeen, Mary.
   Trucks / by Mary Lindeen.
      p. cm. — (Blastoff! Readers) (Mighty machines)
Summary: "Simple text and supportive full-color photographs introduce young readers to trucks. Intended for kindergarten through third grade"—Provided by publisher.
   Includes bibliographical references and index.
   ISBN-13: 978-1-60014-063-1 (hardcover : alk. paper)
   ISBN-10: 1-60014-063-7 (hardcover : alk. paper)
   1. Trucks—Pictorial works—Juvenile literature. I. Title.
TL230.15.L55 2007
629.224—dc22   2006035265

Contents

Big trucks and small trucks drive down the road.

Trucks have a **cab**. The driver sits in the cab.

Trucks have a place for **cargo**. The cargo in this **pickup truck** is hay.

Some very big trucks are called **big rigs**. This big rig has 18 wheels.

This **dump truck** can carry big rocks or dirt.

This **flatbed truck** can carry another truck.

This **logging truck** can carry a big load of logs.

This **tanker truck** can carry milk.

This **monster truck** can race other trucks. On your marks, get set, go!

Glossary

big rig—a very big truck that pulls a trailer

cab—the place where the driver sits in a truck

cargo—loads carried by trucks, ships, trains, or planes

dump truck—a truck with an open body that can be tilted to empty its load

flatbed truck—a truck that pulls a flat trailer

logging truck—a truck that carries logs

monster truck—a pickup truck that has very big wheels

pickup truck—a truck with an open body and small sides

tanker truck—a truck that carries liquids in a tank

To Learn More

AT THE LIBRARY

Coffelt, Nancy. *Pug in a Truck*. New York: Houghton Mifflin, 2006.

Collicutt, Paul. *This Truck*. New York: Farrar Straus Giroux, 2004.

Gordon, David. *The Three Little Rigs*. New York: Laura Geringer, 2005.

ON THE WEB

Learning more about mighty machines is as easy as 1, 2, 3.

1. Go to www.factsurfer.com

2. Enter "mighty machines" into search box.

3. Click the "Surf" button and you will see a list of related web sites.

With factsurfer.com, finding more information is just a click away.

Index